Budget Cooking for One

Vegetarian Dishes

From the Series of Books:

Budget Recipes for One – The Art of Cooking for Yourself

© All Rights Reserved 2014

1

DISCLAIMER

All information in the book is for general information purposes only.

The author has used her best efforts in preparing this information and makes no representations or warranties with respect to the accuracy, applicability or completeness of the material contained within.

Furthermore, the author takes no responsibility for any errors, omissions or inaccuracies in this document. The author disclaims any implied or expressed warranties or fitness for any particular purpose.

The author shall in no event be held liable for losses or damages whatsoever. The author assumes no responsibility or liability for any consequences resulting directly or indirectly from any action or lack of action that you take based on the information in this document.

Use of the publication and recipes therein is at your own risk.

Reproduction or translation of any part of this publication by any means, electronic or mechanical, without the permission of the author, is both forbidden and illegal. You are not permitted to share, sell, and trade or give away this document and it is for your own personal use only, unless stated otherwise.

By using any of the recipes in this publication, you agree that you have read the disclaimer and agree with all the terms.

The reader assumes full risk and responsibility for all actions taken as a result of the information contained within this book and the author will not be held responsible for any loss or damage, whether consequential, incidental, or otherwise that may result from the information presented in this book.

The author has relied on her own experiences when compiling this book and each recipe is tried and tested in her own kitchen.

A couple of the recipes in this book are also included in the authors book

Budget Cooking for One – Supper Dishes

but it was felt that they are also relevant to this book.

(To buy this book simply type the title and authors name into Amazon's search bar)

Table of Contents

4

Introduction

Cooking for a vegetarian can sometimes be a challenge. Thinking of something new and interesting to cook that doesn't include meat or meat products can really test your imagination, especially when cooking for one.

It can be very tempting to resort to the ready-made meals that you can find in the supermarkets. But it really is so much more fun to plan and cook your very own vegetarian food. Cooking for one means you are free to experiment with ingredients and flavors that you particularly like.

No-one wants to eat the same few things week after week so I decided to delve into the selection of recipes I have tried, tested and tweaked over the years and put them into this book.

Some are really quick to put together, others may take a little more time. But all have ingredients that are mostly cheap to buy and easy to find. A lot of the recipes show interesting ways to use left-overs too.

Where possible I have used fresh, seasonal

produce unless there is a good alternative. For example, I would never spend time shelling peas (life is too short...) when I have a bag of frozen peas in the freezer, I also use frozen sweetcorn kernels rather than buying a can that I have to use up.

You may be looking at this book because you have a family member that is vegetarian and you are struggling to come up with good, satisfying meal ideas. You may have a child that has decided not to eat meat anymore for whatever reason (it happens...). You may even have decided to remove meat products from your own diet. Whatever the reason, this book will provide you with some ideas for quick, cheap, nutritious and tasty vegetarian dishes for one as well as stimulate your imagination so you can invent your own.

I have included some fish dishes but appreciate that not all vegetarians eat fish so I have added a couple of bonus recipes to this book – there are 48 recipes instead of the usual 45 that make up my other books.

I would encourage you to be creative and add extras to the recipes in this book. You may have vegetables that need using up so add them to your dish. Add different herbs and spices to see what tickles your taste buds.

The recipes in this book are for one person but, to cook for more people, simply increase the ingredients accordingly.

If you are cooking for one I would advise you to plan a weekly menu; this will help to save you money and minimize waste.

For example, you may fancy trying a veggie curry that uses half a can of coconut milk, so make that recipe on Monday saving the remaining coconut milk for Wednesday when you can try veggies satay skewers.

Or if you find, as I do, that buying peppers in a pack of three is so much cheaper than buying a single pepper, create your weekly menu so you use up the peppers. You could have Stuffed Peppers one day and Battered Peppers with Herb Dip on another day and use the remaining peppers in a stir fry or rice salad.

I have included a couple of recipes that include more expensive ingredients but they are really worth trying occasionally.

Above all, have fun cooking!

I hope this 'Budget Cooking for One – Vegetarian Dishes' cook book helps you to create interesting, cheap and mouthwatering meals that you will enjoy preparing and eating.

Store Cupboard Essentials

The following few pages are included in my first book 'Budget Cooking for One – Supper dishes' but is equally as relevant for this vegetarian recipe book.

Your store cupboard will, over time, come to contain many of the ingredients you will need to try a new recipe.

Make it a habit to buy one item to add to your store cupboard each time you go to the supermarket. That way it won't cost a fortune but you will quickly build up a stash of staple ingredients for lots of recipes. Another thing that I have started to do is to grow some herbs in a window box on the kitchen windowsill. I grow chives, parsley, coriander and oregano at the moment and intend to grow more. It's really easy – even for a house plant killer such as myself...

Below is a list of things that I routinely have in my store cupboard but you may have other ingredients that you want to add.

Seasonings

Sea Salt
Black pepper
White pepper
Dried Herbs
Dried Spices

Dried Chili
Curry powder
Mustard Powder

Cans

Tomatoes
Tuna
Sweetcorn
Coconut Milk
Beans – baked beans, butter beans, kidney beans etc.

Bottles

Honey
Peanut Butter
Vinegar
Red or (and) White Wine Vinegar
Vegetable oil
Olive Oil
Extra Virgin Olive Oil
Tomato Ketchup
Mayonnaise
Soy Sauce
Worcestershire Sauce
Mustard
Chopped Garlic

Dry Stuff

Flour
Pasta – all types
Oats
Rice – long grain, pudding and risotto

Noodles – egg and rice
Stock Cubes
Dried Mushrooms

Fridge

Crème Fraiche
Eggs
Milk
Cheese

Freezer

Vegetables – Peas, Green Beans, Sweetcorn
etc.
Berries – Raspberries, Strawberries,
Gooseberries etc.
Bread – Part Baked and Sliced Shop Bought

Don't underestimate the usefulness of your
freezer. These days frozen vegetables are
just as nutritious as fresh ones and bread
can be taken and used one or two slices at a
time. You may also need to freeze any
leftover soups and recipes you have made
and divided to save for another day.

Cooking for one will sometimes mean that
you may open something and not need to
use the whole package. If the product does
not lend itself to freezing in the raw state,
make another dish to use it up and freeze for
another day. For instance, if I use half a can
of chopped tomatoes I usually make a quick

tomato sauce and freeze to put with a ragu or pasta later.

A lot of recipes use some sort of stock. If you don't have any fresh stock available, use a stock cube or if the recipe just needs a couple of tablespoons of stock cut the cube in half and wrap the other half up in foil to save for another day.

It is so easy to get stuck in a rut and make the same few meals over and over. So try and vary your meals by compiling a weekly menu, making a list of the ingredients you will need and shopping at the beginning of each week.

You will begin to look forward to mealtimes when you know that you will be having something different, nutritious, quick and simple to make and exactly to your own taste.

Remember, variety is the spice of life and you should make sure that a lot of your variety is in your diet.

Vegetarian Dishes

The following pages contain a selection of tried and tested vegetarian dishes that are easy to prepare, economical and very tasty. An added bonus is that many of them are easily adaptable so you can add your own favorite ingredients.

Roasted Pepper and Leek Soup

This is the easiest and tastiest soup to make that I know. It takes a few minutes to prepare the ingredients, a few minutes to blend and it tastes great!

So if time is an issue, this is the soup for you.

Ingredients

1 Red Pepper
1 Yellow Pepper
1 Leek
1 Shallot
1 clove garlic
Milk
Olive oil
Seasoning

Method

The ingredients listed make two or three portions and the soup will keep in the fridge for about 4 days or you could freeze a portion for later.

Remove top, seeds and white core from inside the peppers, cut into four and place on baking tray. Chop leek, garlic and shallot and add to tray.

Drizzle olive oil over the vegetables and shake the tray to ensure everything is covered. Season and place in middle of oven (180°) for around 15 minutes or until vegetables are soft.

You could add some herbs or spices to the tray if you want to jazz it up a little. Coriander or parsley goes particularly well with this soup and you would just add a handful of the fresh herb to the blender.

When the vegetables are cooked, tip everything into a blender, add a little milk and blend until smooth. Add as much milk as needed to reach your desired consistency.

Serve with a swirl of cream or crème fraiche and some crusty bread.

Delicious!

Mushroom and Spinach Pasta

This is what I would call vegetarian 'comfort food'. It is quick and easy to make and, if you are a fan of creamy pasta, this is the ultimate supper dish.

Ingredients

224g (8oz) dried penne pasta
1 tablespoon olive oil
112g (4oz) mushrooms
1 clove garlic (optional)
1 teaspoon dried oregano
100ml (4 fl oz) vegetable stock
1 dessertspoon lemon juice
2-3 tablespoon cream cheese
112g (4oz) fresh or frozen spinach
Seasoning

Method

Cook pasta according to packet instructions. Drain, reserve 50ml (2 fl oz) of the cooking liquid.

Meanwhile, slice the mushrooms and garlic (if using). Heat oil in a frying pan and add the garlic and mushrooms. Cook for 4-5 minutes, stirring frequently. Stir in the oregano, lemon juice and stock and cook for a further 7-8 minutes or until reduced.

Stir in the cream cheese and spinach and cook over a low heat for 2-4 minutes.
Add the reserved cooking liquid; you can add it all or just a little – your choice, then the cooked pasta. Stir well to combine.

Taste and season. Serve with a few parmesan shavings and garlic bread.

Baked Brie and Sweet Onion Chutney with Beetroot Salad

This is a simple dish that can be a lovely starter or just as nice on your lap in front of the TV.

Ingredients

Brie
Jar of Sweet Onion
Chutney
1 Cooked Beetroot
Teaspoon Parmesan

Method

Slice the brie and arrange the slices in a small ovenproof ramekin. Add a spoonful of sweet onion chutney then add more brie. Repeat until the ramekin is just over ¾ full. Place in preheated medium oven for around 10 minutes or until bubbling and golden.

Meanwhile cut the beetroot into small cubes, toss in vinaigrette and arrange on plate with a selection of leaves dressed with the same light vinaigrette.

When the brie is cooked add another spoonful of sweet onion chutney and sprinkle with the parmesan.

Serve immediately with buttered crusty bread for dipping into the brie.

Note: You could use Camembert or any other cheese of that type.

Quick Beetroot Soup

Simple to make and a favorite of mine.

Ingredients

2 Cooked Beetroots
1 Carrot
1 Onion
1 Stick of Celery
½ pint Vegetable Stock
Small knob of Butter
Seasoning

Method

Cut up and cook carrot, onion and celery in the vegetable stock until soft. Grate the beetroot and add to the pan keeping a little back to add later for a bit of texture. Simmer for 2 minutes until the cooked beetroot is hot.

Put your soup in a blender and blitz to the desired consistency adding extra stock if needed.

Taste and season.

Put back in saucepan with the rest of the grated beetroot to reheat. Add butter and stir well.

Serve with a swirl of cream or crème fraîche and some warm crusty bread – delicious!

Cheese Potato and Onion Croquettes

A lovely side dish for a nut roast or a large green salad.

Ingredients

224g (8oz) potatoes - mashed
28g (1oz) butter
1 small onion or shallot
74g (3oz) your choice of cheese - grated
1 tablespoon plain flour
1 beaten egg
Dried breadcrumbs
Enough vegetable oil to deep fry

Method

Peel and finely chop the onion. Melt the butter over a gentle heat and add the onion. Fry gently until the onion is softened but not browned.

Tip the onion and butter into the mashed potatoes, add the grated cheese and mix well. Place in fridge for 10 minutes to chill.

Divide the mixture into 4 and roll into croquettes. Chill in freezer for 15 minutes.

Spread the flour on a plate, put the beaten egg on a flat place and spread the breadcrumbs on another plate. Cover the croquettes in the flour, then the egg before rolling in the breadcrumbs.

Heat the oil until a cube of white bread takes 45-55 seconds to brown. Fry the croquettes until golden brown.

Drain on kitchen paper.

Note: There are lots of variations on this theme but it is a quick way to use up leftover mashed potatoes. For instance you could substitute the cheese for chopped nuts or hard boiled eggs.

Potato Patties

These potato patties are great for using up left-over mashed potatoes and vegetables. They will freeze well and are a great accompaniment for bacon or sausages for meat eaters, but are just as nice with a fresh green salad.

Ingredients

Left over mashed potatoes
Any left-over vegetables
Flour
1 beaten egg
Butter and olive oil to cook.

Optional

Handful of grated cheese

Method

Put potatoes in large bowl, add beaten egg and vegetables (optional; will be just as nice plain). Mix together thoroughly.

Add enough flour to bring the mixture to a

firm dough.

Divide into patties about 4 inches across and as thick as you want them to be.

Shallow fry until golden brown on both sides. Excellent for Sunday Brunch served with tomatoes and baked beans.

You can also add a handful of finely chopped herbs to ring the changes.

Wrap any surplus patties individually and freeze for later.

Note: For the non-vegetarian in the family try frying some bacon until crispy and add instead of vegetables – another treat for breakfast.

Mushroom Risotto

This is a very simple recipe and the mushrooms can be replaced with anything you happen to have in the fridge.

Ingredients

Tablespoon of olive oil
Knob of butter
Small onion
1 clove of garlic
Hot Vegetable Stock
140g (5oz) Risotto rice
Small handful of frozen garden peas (optional)

Small handful sweetcorn kernels (optional)
Mushrooms – any variety (a small amount is fine)
Small handful of Parmesan or any grated cheese.
Salt and pepper

Method

Heat the oil and butter in a frying pan and add the onions and garlic. Fry gently until the onion is transparent and soft. Stir in the mushrooms and cook for a few minutes.

Add the risotto rice and stir until the rice is well combined with the vegetables, butter and oil.

Begin to add the stock, a ladleful at a time, stirring thoroughly. Stir until the stock is absorbed before adding more. Keep adding the stock a ladleful at a time until the rice is soft but with a little bite. The risotto should be creamy.

Add peas and sweetcorn stir in well. Remove from heat, stir and season. Serve immediately; sprinkle with the grated cheese just before eating.

Spicy Veggie Burgers

These burgers are great hot or cold and can be safely frozen for up to a month. You could even pop one or two in your lunchbox.

Ingredients

1 small can chickpeas
1 carrot
2 shallots
28g (1oz) chopped pine nuts (or your own choice of nuts)
1 clove garlic
Fresh coriander
1 teaspoon chili powder (you can omit this if you don't want 'spicy')
1 teaspoon paprika

Method

Preheat the oven to around 200° or Gas 6.

Place all the ingredients in a food processor and blend for 10 seconds. Open the lid and push the ingredients down before blending again. Repeat until the mixture is the consistency you prefer (chunky or smooth) but thick enough to form a ball.

Using wet hands to stop the mixture sticking, form the mixture into golf ball sized balls and place on a baking tray lined with baking parchment.

Flatten the balls slightly to form a burger shape and bake for around 20 minutes until golden brown. Leave to cool for a few minutes before removing from the tray.

Serve with a few healthy fries and fresh garden peas.

Healthy Fries

Cut potatoes into thin strips and wash thoroughly. Pat dry and arrange on baking tray. Spray with olive oil and bake in moderate oven, turning the potatoes a few times, until crisp and golden.

One Pan Breakfast Omelet

Ideal for supper or breakfast. Double the quantities to share with your friends. Cooks altogether in one pan so saves on washing up – always a good thing according to my kids!

Ingredients

1 or 2 eggs
1 large tomato
2 or 3 mushrooms
Sliced red pepper
Dessertspoon of milk
Small amount of oil for cooking
Seasoning

Method

Cook tomato, mushroom and pepper in the oil in a frying pan. Set aside.

Beat the egg and milk together well, add seasoning.

Pour into the hot frying pan then return the tomato, mushroom and pepper to the pan. Swirl the egg mixture around the pan until it starts to cook. Allow to cook until the underside of the omelet is golden brown. Flip the omelet and cook for a further minute or two. Alternatively, instead of flipping your omelet you can pop the pan under a hot grill to cook the top.

Serve immediately with baked beans and a slice of hot toast. Delicious!

Vegetable Medley Italian Style

The only limit on this dish is your own imagination. This is something I regularly make when I have lots of bits of vegetables left over – usually at the end of the week.

Ingredients

224g (8oz) plum tomatoes
1 small onion
1 clove garlic
1 zucchini
100ml vegetable stock
1 dessertspoon tomato puree
1 tablespoon fresh oregano
Seasoning
Parmesan (optional)
1 tablespoon toasted flaked almonds
Any other vegetables you have

Method

Skin the tomatoes by putting a cross in the tops of the tomatoes and cover with boiling water. Allow to stand for a minute or two. Remove then plunge into cold water. The skins should be easy to remove. Roughly chop the flesh.

Peel the onion and cut into wedges. Peel and crush the garlic. Slice the zucchini and any other vegetables you have chosen to use.

Heat the stock in a pan then add the garlic, vegetables, tomato puree and fresh herbs. Cover pan and simmer for around 15 minutes until vegetables are tender.

Remove the lid and boil for 4 minutes or until the liquid is reduced and thickened. Turn out into your serving dish. Sprinkle the toasted almonds over the vegetables, garnish with a sprinkle of parmesan and some fresh oregano. Serve immediately.

Easy Spaghetti Bolognese

No need for a jar of ready-made sauce where you would waste half when making half portions – it's just as simple to make your own sauce designed just how you like it.

Ingredients

Mushrooms – as many or as few as you like
I small onion or 2 shallots
Small amount of oil
Can of chopped tomatoes
2 cloves garlic
Any herbs you like
Small red chili, chopped (optional)
Spaghetti
Black pepper for seasoning

Optional

Grated parmesan cheese

Method

Fry the onion, chopped chili and garlic if using, gently in the oil until soft and transparent. Add the mushrooms and fry for 2 minutes.

Pour in the can of chopped tomatoes and bring to the boil. Turn the heat down and simmer for 10 minutes. Add any herbs you want – basil or oregano is very tasty. Stir well, taste and season to your liking.

Whilst the sauce is cooking add your spaghetti to a large saucepan of boiling water and cook until soft but still with a bit of 'bite'. Pour through a colander to drain liquid then pour over some boiling water to prevent the spaghetti from sticking together.

Put the spaghetti in a large bowl and add the sauce. Toss until all the spaghetti is coated. Tip onto your serving plate then garnish with grated parmesan and a few fresh herbs.

Serve with a few pieces of hot garlic bread.

Garlic Bread

This is an easy and delicious way to use up any bread that is going a bit hard or rolls that have been around for a day or two.

Ingredients

Couple of slices of crusty bread
Garlic
Good olive oil

Method

Place bread in frying pan with oil and fry on both sides until crisp and golden.
Remove from pan, drizzle with olive oil and rub peeled garlic over both sides whilst still quite warm.

Or

Take about 50g of soft butter, add crushed the garlic and mix together well. Leave in the fridge for an hour or two to make it easier to work with.

Make cuts along the top of a crusty roll, not quite cutting through. Insert the garlic butter in the cuts and place in medium oven for about 5 minutes.

Simple Small Savory Pastries

These mini pastries are great for adding to a lunchbox or a picnic. Also great with a few French fries for supper.

Ingredients

112g (4oz) frozen puff pastry
2 eggs
75ml (3 fl oz) milk
56g (2oz) mature Cheddar cheese
1 beef tomato (or as large as you can find)
Seasoning
Butter for greasing the tray

Method

Preheat your oven to 200°C, 400°F, Gas Mark 6. Grease a deep 6 hole muffin tin.

Roll the pastry out on a lightly floured surface until it is very thin. Cut out as many rounds as you can get to fit the muffin tin, making sure the pastry comes just above the top of the hole in the muffin tin.

Beat the eggs and milk together in a jug and season. Divide the cheese between the pastry cases then pour the egg mixture over. Top each with a slice of tomato.

Bake in the oven for around 20 minutes or until risen and golden colored.

Cheese Twists

These cheese twists are ideal for using up any left-over puff pastry after making the Savory Pastries on the previous page.

Ingredients

85g (3oz) Gruyere cheese
½ teaspoon paprika
375g (13oz) ready made puff pastry
1 beaten egg
Butter to grease baking tray

Method

Preheat the oven to 200C, 400F, Gas Mark 6 and grease a large baking sheet.

Mix together cheese and paprika, roll out the pastry and sprinkle cheese and paprika over. Fold the pastry in half and roll again to the required thickness.

Cut the pastry into 1cm (½ inch) wide strips then cut each strip in half and gently twist. Put onto the greased baking sheet and brush with the beaten egg.

Bake in the preheated oven for 8-10 minutes or until crisp and golden. Cool on a wire rack and store in airtight container

Battered Peppers with Herb Dip

These are really good for a TV snack or served with a huge salad for lunch. You are not limited to peppers, you could use zucchinis, leeks, part cooked parsnips or carrots – use your imagination!

Ingredients

2 tablespoons flour
1 small egg
100ml beer
2 red peppers or a mixture of your choice of vegetables
1 dessertspoon ground coriander
Vegetable oil for deep frying

For the Garlic Dip

1 clove garlic
Coriander
Parsley
Chives
112g (4oz) mayonnaise
Seasoning

Method

Mix the flour and ground coriander in a bowl and season well. Make a well in the center and drop in the egg. Start whisking whilst adding the beer until a smooth batter is achieved. Set aside in the fridge for at least 30 minutes.

Deseed peppers and cut into strips. If you are using other vegetables cut them into strips.

Peel and crush the garlic, finely chop the fresh herbs. Put the chopped herbs, garlic and mayonnaise in a bowl, add salt and pepper and mix until well combined. Taste and adjust the seasoning if required. Cover and keep in fridge until required.

Half fill a pan with oil and heat until a square of bread browns in under a minute. Dip the vegetables into the batter to coat and drop carefully into the oil. Deep fry for 2-3 minutes or until golden. You may have to fry your vegetables in batches to avoid overfilling the pan.

Drain well on kitchen paper, keep warm until all vegetables are deep fried. Serve with the chilled herb dip.

Simple Homemade Pizza

This simple pizza can be prepared in a few minutes. You can use up ingredients that you already have in your fridge and store cupboard. For example, most people will have tomato ketchup in the cupboard so you don't need to buy tomato puree and there are usually a few tomatoes and bits of cheese that need using up. Left over vegetables are great to use too. Be inventive!

Ingredients

1 packet of frozen puff pastry
Tomato puree or tomato ketchup
Grated cheese
Topping of your choice
Few basil leaves (optional)

Method

Defrost puff pastry and cut in two. Wrap and refreeze one half for another time.

Roll out the puff pastry to around the thickness of a coin – square or circle; it doesn't matter. Place onto a baking tray.

Draw a line around the edge of your pastry base with a sharp knife about 1 inch from the edge without cutting through the pastry.

Squeeze about 2 inches of tomato puree or tablespoon of tomato ketchup onto the center of the base and spread evenly up to the scored line using the back of a spoon. Add grated cheese then your choice of topping. Tomatoes, ham (I'm not a strict vegetarian; I just love veggie food) and leftover vegetables are my favorite. Sprinkle with a little more cheese and the basil leaves (if used).

Cook in the middle of oven using the temperature guide on the pastry packet. Cook until the pastry is crisp and golden around the edge of your pizza. Drizzle a little extra virgin olive oil over the pizza and serve immediately.

Note: You could use pitta bread for the pizza base if you prefer a crispy pizza. Simply open up the pitta bread and use as above.

Creamy Mushroom Muffins

A fabulous quick and easy snack for eating in front of the TV or an impressive starter if served on blinis.

Ingredients

224g (8oz) button mushrooms
2 shallots
1 clove garlic
28g (1oz) butter
1 dessertspoon olive oil
100ml (4 fl oz) double cream
Pinch grated nutmeg
Seasoning
1 dessertspoon chopped fresh parsley plus a few sprigs to garnish
2 plain bread muffins
2 tablespoons Madeira wine (optional)

Method

Slice the mushrooms, peel and finely chop the shallots and garlic. Heat the oil and butter in a frying pan. Add the shallots and garlic and fry for 3-4 minutes until softened.

Add mushrooms to pan and fry for a further 3-4 minutes, stirring occasionally. Add the Madeira if you are using and boil rapidly for a few seconds. Reduce the heat and stir in the cream. Add the nutmeg and season.

Cook for 2 minutes turning the heat up for the final minute so the sauce thickens. Stir in the chopped parsley.

Toast the muffins and spoon the mushroom mixture over then garnish with more parsley.

Serve immediately.

Speedy Tomato Soup

Although this recipe is for tomato soup, you can use this method to make mushroom, vegetable, parsnip, broccoli or leek and potato soup. Simply omit the sugar from the recipe and cook vegetables until soft.

Ingredients

6 medium tomatoes
Milk or mixture of milk and cream
1 clove garlic
Olive oil
1 teaspoon sugar
Salt and pepper
Herbs if desired (oregano is particularly good with tomaotes)
Grated cheese for serving

Method

Coat the tomatoes in the olive oil and place on baking tray. Crush the garlic and add to the tray. Shake the tray a few times before placing in the middle of a hot oven to roast – about 15 minutes.

Remove from oven and tip everything into a blender, add any herbs you are using. Add the sugar and a little bit of milk and blitz. Keep adding the milk until your soup reaches the desired consistency. Put into saucepan and reheat. Taste and season.

Pour into bowl and sprinkle a little grated cheese over the top if using or you could swirl a spoonful of cream or crème fraiche through the soup before serving. Serve with garlic croutons.

Note: Garlic croutons are quick and easy to make. Cut left over bread into small even squares. Crush and fry one clove of garlic in butter until softened. Add a little more butter along with the cubes of bread and fry gently on all sides until crisp and golden. Drain on kitchen paper. These croutons will freeze for use later. I always have a tub of croutons in the freezer.

Asparagus Tips with Cheese Sauce

I know asparagus is a little bit more expensive but it is worth the extra to treat yourself to a bunch when it is in season. You could use some for this recipe and make the remainder into a delicious soup (see later in the book).

Ingredients

6 Asparagus tips

For the sauce:

28g (1oz) butter
28g (1oz) flour
Milk
Grated cheese

Method

Cook the asparagus in boiling salted water for around 3 minutes or until just softening.

Melt the butter in a saucepan over a medium heat then add the flour, stirring continuously with a wooden spoon. It will look lumpy at first but it will come together; so don't panic!

Once the flour and butter are mixed together to a paste, begin to add the milk a bit at a time, stirring all the time. The mixture will thicken each time you add milk. Keep adding more milk whilst stirring until the sauce reaches your desired thickness (I like mine quite thick). Add as much grated cheese as you like until it tastes good to you. Stir in well. Taste and season.

Drain the asparagus well and place side-by-side in an oven proof dish. Pour the cheese sauce over the top and sprinkle with a little grated cheese. Place under grill to until browned and bubbling.

Delicious served with a few new potatoes.

Devilled Egg Salad Supper

A lovely, quick to prepare, light supper to eat in front of the TV.

Ingredients

2 eggs
Mayonnaise
Knob of butter
Dash of
Worcestershire
sauce
Paprika (or grated gruyere cheese)

Your choice of salad ingredients, for example:

Watercress
Tomatoes
Chopped peppers
Rocket leaves
Sweetcorn
Salad dressing
Etc..

Method

Put the eggs in a saucepan of cold water and boil for around 8 minutes. Drain and place eggs into a bowl of cold water.

When cold remove the shells and, using a sharp knife, cut each egg in half lengthways.

Scoop the yolks out into a bowl. Add butter, mayonnaise (I quite often substitute the mayonnaise for salad cream) and Worcestershire sauce. Mix together using a fork until smooth and well combined.

Spoon the mixture back into the egg whites and sprinkle with paprika (I sometime omit the paprika and use a bit of grated gruyere cheese and melt under the grill).

Serve with your salad and a wedge of buttered crusty bread.

Switch on your favorite TV program and enjoy.

Note: Try adding a few finely chopped herbs to the mixture before spooning back into the egg whites – delicious!

Tacos with Caramelized Potatoes and Tomatoes

Make lots to share with friends or just a couple for a TV snack.

Ingredients

Taco shells
Handful of baby new potatoes
2 or 3 tomatoes
28g (1oz) butter
100ml vegetable stock
1 red onion
1 clove garlic
1 dessertspoon of demerara sugar

Method

Wash the potatoes and cut in half. Place in pan with butter and stock and cook until softened.

Meanwhile peel and chop onion and garlic. Add to pan of potatoes and cook for a further 10 minutes. Chop tomatoes and add to pan, cook for another 5 minutes. If there is still liquid in the pan turn the heat up high and cook until evaporated.

Sprinkle with the sugar and cook over a low heat for a few minutes until the sugar has thickened.

Spoon the mixture into taco shells, garnish with a spoonful of crème fraiche and a couple of mint leaves and serve.

Note: For a lovely summer snack, fill your taco shells with iceberg lettuce, avocado, tomato and top with sour cream.

Easy Tuna Omelet

Everyone has a can of tuna lurking in the back of the store cupboard. Here is a tasty way to use it.

Ingredients

2 fresh eggs
Knob of butter
Small can of tuna chunks in oil
Tablespoon of chopped mushrooms
Tablespoon of frozen sweetcorn
56g (2oz) Greek-style yoghurt
Salt and pepper

Method

Whisk eggs, add salt and pepper.

Drain the oil from the can of tuna into an omelet pan. Add mushrooms and sweetcorn, fry for 2 minutes. Add tuna and fry for a further minute. Stir in the yoghurt and cook until warmed through.

Remove mixture from pan and keep warm.

Wipe the pan with kitchen paper then melt the butter over a medium heat. Add the beaten eggs. Cook for around 3 minutes or until set. Remember not to stir or the eggs will scramble but occasionally draw in the edge with a wooden spatula to allow any uncooked egg to run underneath.

Top one half of the omelet with the tuna mixture. Fold over to enclose the filling. Serve immediately with a green salad or a few French fries.

Easy Asparagus Soup

This is a really easy and tasty soup – you should really try it when asparagus is in season. It is a lovely pale green color and tastes  beautiful and creamy. To serve as a starter for a dinner party, simply increase the ingredients – your guests will be suitably impressed.

Ingredients

8-10 asparagus spears
2 shallots
28g (1oz) butter
1 clove garlic
1 dessertspoon flour
Seasoning

Method

Chop the asparagus into 5cm (2in) pieces (*you can use the woody bits for the soup and keep the tips to make Asparagus Tips with Cheese Sauce*), place in a pan and cover with plenty of water.

Boil until the asparagus is soft.

Peel and finely chop the shallots and garlic then gently fry in the butter until soft and transparent. Add the flour to the onions and garlic and stir in.

Add the cooking liquid from the asparagus a bit at a time, stirring all the time. The liquid will thicken as you stir. When the soup reaches your preferred thickness add the cooked asparagus and simmer for 2-3 minutes. If you don't have enough cooking liquid simply use water or vegetable stock. Taste and season well with salt and pepper to your liking.

Blend for a minute or two then pass the soup through a sieve to remove any stringy bits.

Reheat and add a few drops of pesto and swirl of cream or crème fraiche before serving.

Tomato Tagliatelle

Another tasty dish that can be prepared in about 15 minutes.

Ingredients

Tagliatelle for one
1 shallot
1 clove garlic
168g (6oz) small tomatoes
112g (4oz) savoy cabbage
1 tablespoon olive oil
2 tablespoons stock – chicken or vegetable
112g (4oz) ricotta cheese
2 tablespoons cream
Grated cheese to garnish – if required

Method

Cook the pasta according to packet instructions, drain and keep warm.

Meanwhile finely chop the shallots, finely shred the cabbage, peel and crush garlic and cut tomatoes into quarters.

Heat oil in frying pan or wok. Add shallots and garlic. Cook until shallots are just softened. Add cabbage and cook for a further 3-4 minutes. Add tomatoes and cook for another 3-4 minutes. Stir in the stock and simmer for 2 minutes.

In a large bowl beat the ricotta cheese and cream together. Add the drained pasta and toss to coat. Add the tomato mixture and toss again to coat the tagliatelle with the mixture.

Serve immediately garnished with the grated cheese if you have chosen to use it.

Sweetcorn Fritters

Serve these fritters with a homemade tomato sauce and a baked potato.

Ingredients

1 red pepper
224g (8oz) button mushrooms
1 tablespoon sweetcorn kernels
1 egg
28g (1oz) butter
50ml milk
56g plain flour
½ teaspoon salt
½ teaspoon baking powder
1 dessertspoon fresh chopped chives
Vegetable oil to shallow fry
Herb leaves to garnish

Method

Remove seeds and white core from pepper then chop finely. Chop the mushrooms.

Melt the butter in a frying pan over a low heat. Beat egg, milk and melted butter together. Gradually beat in the flour, baking powder and salt until a smooth, thick batter is achieved. Stir in the red pepper, mushrooms, sweetcorn and chives.

Heat ½ inch (1 cm) of oil in the pan over a high heat. Reduce heat and carefully drop spoonfuls of the mixture into the pan leaving space for the fritters to spread. Cook for 2 minutes each side or until the fritters are puffy and golden brown.

Remove fritters from the pan and drain well on kitchen paper. Repeat until all batter is used.

Serve hot garnished with fresh herb leaves.

Individual Sweet Onion and Goats Cheese Tarts

These individual tarts are ideal for a quick and easy supper served with a green salad or a few boiled new potatoes. They look like you have spent ages making them so are great to produce when you have company. Honestly – ANYONE can make these in minutes!

Ingredients

Packet of shortcrust pastry (or you could make your own)
Jar of sweet onion chutney
Goat's cheese – easiest if you buy the goat's cheese in a roll.
Parsley to garnish
Small tart tins

Method

Lightly grease your tart tins.

Roll out your pastry to the thickness of a coin and line each tart tin carefully. Cover with greaseproof paper and fill with baking beans or dried peas to stop the pastry from rising (called baking blind). Cook in a pre-heated oven 180° until the edges are just beginning to brown.

Remove from oven and allow to cool slightly.

Cut goat's cheese into circles (if you bought a roll) or bite sized pieces. Take a spoonful of the onion chutney and spread over the base of your tart then put the goat's cheese on top. Add a little more onion chutney to the top of the cheese; you could also add a few slices of tomato if you like. Return to oven to bake – about 8-10 minutes.

You can serve these either hot or cold with a little chopped parsley sprinkled over each.

Note: These are even nicer made with filo pastry. But if you are using shortcrust pastry and you don't have any individual tart tins you could simple cut your pastry into small squares and pinch the four corners so they stand up. Small squares will work better in this case. Then bake blind and fill as before.

Crisp Vegetable Tempura

This recipe sounds very technical but is really very simple to make. A great dish to make for a snack in front of the TV.

The vegetables listed are just suggestions but you can use any vegetables you like.

Ingredients

For the batter:

84g (3oz) cornflour
56g (2oz) plain flour
2 teaspoons baking powder
1 teaspoon semolina
1 teaspoon mustard powder
½ teaspoon salt
Water

Vegetables

1 zucchini
1 small red onion
1 pepper – any color
Mange tout
Baby sweetcorn
1 small leek
Oil for deep frying

Method

Cut vegetables into slices then place on kitchen paper to dry.

Mix together cornflour, baking powder, flour, mustard powder, salt and semolina. Beat in around ½ pint of very cold water to make a thick batter.

Heat the oil in a deep pan until a cube of bread turns golden in 1 minute. Dip the vegetable pieces in the batter until evenly coated, wiping the excess off on the edge of the batter dish. Deep fry in the oil for around 3-4 minutes or until crisp and golden.

Drain on kitchen paper. Repeat until all vegetables are done. Serve immediately.

Cheesy Stuffed Potato Skins

Again, another very simple dish. The only problem you will face is choosing what to stuff the potato skins with if you want to ring the changes. But for the purpose of this recipe we will concentrate on the cheesy filling.

Ingredients

2 medium sized potatoes
Cream cheese
Small onion
Butter
1 tablespoon of oil
1 clove garlic if desired
Grated cheese.

Method

Place the potatoes in the microwave and cook until nearly soft inside. Next place in a hot oven to complete the baking and crisp the skins.

Meanwhile, chop the onion and garlic (if used) and fry in the oil until soft and transparent. Drain way any excess oil.

Remove potatoes from oven and, using a sharp knife, cut in half lengthways. Being careful with the hot potatoes, scoop the insides of the potatoes out into a bowl. Add the butter, onion, garlic and a handful of grated cheese. Mash together well.

Place the empty skins on a lightly greased baking tray and spread a little cream cheese over the inside of each skin.

Fill each skin with the cheesy potato mixture and top with a sprinkling of grated cheese. You could also add a slice of tomato or a sprinkling of chopped chives to the top of each at this stage.

Return to oven and bake until the cheese is melted and golden brown. Serve with a crisp green salad.

Mushrooms with Leek Sauce

This is a lovely creamy mushroom dish and is quick and easy to prepare.

Ingredients

8-10 mixed mushrooms
1 large leek
56g (2oz) butter
1 clove garlic
1 dessertspoon wholegrain mustard
Small glass dry white wine or 3 tablespoons vegetable stock
2 tablespoons crème fraiche

Method

Peel and crush the garlic. Trim leeks and cut into 1cm thick slices.

Melt the butter in a pan and add the garlic. Fry gently for a minute or two then add the mushrooms. Stir in the leeks, mustard and wine (or stock).

Bring the mixture to the boil adding a little water if necessary. Reduce the heat, cover and simmer for around 5-8 minutes.

Stir the crème fraiche into the pan. Taste and season to your liking. Serve immediately with some creamy mashed potatoes or baby new potatoes.

Note: When using wine in cooking, only use wine that you would drink yourself. If you wouldn't drink a glass of it yourself, the taste would not improve in any dish.

Cheese and Potato Balls

I love these with just a small dish of tomato ketchup or a dish of melted camembert cheese. But just as delicious with a salad.

Ingredients

2 potatoes
56g (2oz) Cheddar Cheese
28g (1oz) butter
28g (1oz) plain flour
1 egg
Pinch of grated nutmeg
Vegetable oil to deep fry
Grated Parmesan and Paprika to garnish

Method

Peel and dice the potatoes. Cook in a pan of salted boiling water until soft. Drain and mash until smooth. Allow to cool.

Grate the cheese. Melt the butter in a pan and stir in 3 tablespoons of water. Remove pan from heat and stir in the flour beating the mixture well until it forms a smooth ball. Beat the eggs and add them gradually to the flour mixture until smooth and glossy. Stir in the nutmeg, cheddar cheese and potatoes.

Taste and season well.

Fill a deep pan with the oil until one third full. Heat oil until a cube of bread dropped into the oil takes 1 minute to brown. Drop 2 – 3 dessertspoonfuls of the potato mixture into the pan *carefully*.

Deep fry for 3 – 4 minutes turning once, until puffed up and golden. Drain on kitchen paper and keep hot. Repeat until you have used up your mixture. Sprinkle with parmesan and paprika.

Serve immediately.

Pancakes with Creamy Leek and Mushroom Stuffing

This is yet another recipe that will allow you to ring the changes with your fillings.

Ingredients

8 – 10 mushrooms
56g (2oz) grated cheddar cheese
1 leek
28g (1oz) butter
28g (1oz) flour
125ml (4 fl oz) milk
Seasoning
3 ready-made pancakes or tortillas

Method

Cut the mushrooms and leek into thin slices.

Melt the butter in a saucepan, add the mushrooms and leek and fry for a couple of minutes until just softened.

Sprinkle in the flour and stir gently to coat the mushrooms and leeks. Add the milk gradually stirring all the time whilst the mixture thickens. Add half the cheese and stir until melted.

Taste and season to your liking.

Preheat the grill. Spoon the mushroom sauce along the center of each pancake and roll up to enclose the filling. Transfer to a shallow ovenproof dish and sprinkle over the remaining cheese. Grill for 3-4 minutes or until golden brown.

Serve immediately with a crunchy green salad dressed with a lemon vinaigrette.

Tomato Noodles with Pesto

Quick and easy supper dish that is a personal favorite of mine.

Ingredients

140g (5oz) noodle of your choice. You can use fettucine, spaghetti, tagliatelle etc.
2 dessertspoons olive oil
224g (8oz) cherry tomatoes
1 clove garlic
1 tablespoon crème fraiche
2 tablespoons green pesto (from a jar or your own home-made)
Seasoning
Watercress for garnish (you could use grated parmesan cheese if you prefer)

Method

Add the pasta and 1 dessertspoon oil to a pan of boiling water and cook according to pasta packet instructions.

Halve the tomatoes, peel and finely chop the garlic.

Heat the remaining oil in a wok or pan. Add garlic and fry for a minute. Add tomatoes and cook for 5 minutes until tomatoes are lightly browned and softened. Remove from heat and stir in crème fraiche. Taste and season to your liking.

Drain the pasta thoroughly and return to pan. Add the pesto and toss to coat.

Pour into a large serving dish and tip the tomato mixture over the top of the pasta.

Garnish with watercress or parmesan and serve immediately.

Vegetables Rice and Pesto Salad

This is a very tasty way to use up any leftover vegetables that you have sitting in your fridge. You could also add any leftover cold meat (chicken, ham etc.) to the salad for the non-vegetarian. This salad is a great picnic dish or good for your lunchbox. The vegetables listed below are simply suggestions; use whatever you have available.

Ingredients

140g (5oz) long grain rice
140g (5oz) cherry tomatoes
Red pepper
Green pepper
Spring onions
Few slices of cucumber
1 clove garlic
Tablespoon pesto
Tablespoon white wine vinegar
1 tablespoon vegetable oil
2 tablespoons good olive oil
Seasoning

Method

Rinse the rice and cook using the 2 to 1 method (2 parts water to 1 part rice). Drain the rice and rinse under cold running water. Transfer to your chosen serving bowl.

Chop your vegetables into small dice. Cook in vegetable oil until soft. Mix into the rice thoroughly.

Peel and crush the clove of garlic. Add the garlic to the pesto, white wine vinegar and olive oil. Whisk until well combined. Drizzle the dressing over the rice salad and toss.

Serve warm or cold.

Creamy Zucchini with Spaghetti

Ingredients

1 zucchini
1 clove garlic
Parmesan cheese
1 tablespoon olive oil
140g (5oz) dried spaghetti
1 dessertspoon crème fraiche
1 dessertspoon fresh shredded basil leaves
Black pepper

Method

Slice the zucchini and peel and crush the garlic. Grate or thinly slice the parmesan cheese.

Heat half the oil in a frying pan and add the zucchinis and garlic. Cook for 3-4 minutes stirring occasionally.

Meanwhile cook the spaghetti as per the packet instructions. Drain well then add to the zucchini. Add the remaining oil and the crème fraiche and toss well. Taste and season to your liking.

Serve topped with parmesan cheese.

Zucchini and Cheese Frittata

I love these; I always make one more than I need because I just *know* I'll eat one right away!

Ingredients

1 zucchini
Grated zest of 1 lemon
2 spring onions
1 clove garlic
56g (2oz) cheddar cheese
1 egg
56g (2oz) plain flour
Vegetable oil to shallow fry
Seasoning

Method

Grate the zucchini into a bowl and add the lemon zest, spring onions, garlic, and cheese. Mix in the egg.

Gradually add the flour mixing all the time. Just use enough to make the mixture into a thick batter. Season with salt and pepper.

Heat the oil in a frying pan over a medium heat. Drop spoonfuls of the mixture into the oil leaving space between them.

Fry over a medium heat for around 3 minutes each side or until nicely golden brown.

Drain on kitchen paper and serve with minted new potatoes and a chili sauce.

Potato Crisps with Lemon and Lime Salsa

A great supper snack. Great to eat in front of the TV with an assortment of dips. The crisps will keep if kept in an airtight container.

Ingredients

For the Salsa:

224g (8oz) ripe tomatoes
Half small onion
1 clove garlic
1 tablespoon fresh coriander
Juice of half lemon
Juice of half lime
1 tablespoon good olive oil
1 teaspoon balsamic vinegar
Chopped chili (optional)
Seasoning

For the Crisps:

Waxy potatoes – as many as you want!
Vegetable oil to deep fry
Salt

Method

To make the Salsa:

Make a cross in the top of each tomato, put in a bowl and pour boiling water over them. Soak for 2 minutes then peel. Remove seeds and chop roughly. Chop onion and coriander.

Mix onion, tomatoes, lime and lemon juice, vinegar, chili (if used), garlic and oil together well. Chill for at least 15 minutes before serving.

To make the Crisps:

Peel the potatoes and slice very thinly. Soak the slices in iced water for at least 15 minutes. Drain and dry thoroughly on a clean tea towel. Half fill a deep pan with the vegetable oil and heat until a cube of bread turns brown in 30 seconds when dropped in. Lower the potato slices carefully into the hot oil a few at a time and deep fry turning frequently, until the slices rise to the top and are golden brown. Remove crisps and drain on kitchen paper. Sprinkle with a little salt. When cold store in an airtight container until you are ready to use.

Note: There are lots of variations for delicious dips to eat with your crisps. Try the Brie and Sweet Onion Chutney recipe or be adventurous and invent one of your own.

Almond Pesto and Pasta

Quick, tasty and simple to make, this pasta dish is great either on its own or served with a tomato salad.

Ingredients

112g (4oz) dried spaghetti
1 clove garlic
84g (3oz) blanched almonds
1 tablespoon fresh basil leaves
3 tablespoons olive oil
Grated parmesan cheese

Method

Cook spaghetti as per the packet instruction being careful not to overcook.

Peel the garlic. Dry fry the nuts in a frying pan for 3-4 minutes tossing until golden brown. Reserve 25g (1oz) of the nuts and put the rest in a food processor. Add the garlic, basil (keeping a few leaves back), oil and cheese. Blend for a few seconds until smooth.

Drain the pasta and return to the pan. Add the almond pesto and toss until the pasta is coated with the sauce.

Using a sharp knife, chop the remaining almonds and sprinkle over the pasta. Taste and season to your liking. Garnish with the reserved basil leaves. Serve immediately with hot garlic bread.

Note: You could add some chopped cooked chicken or a handful of prawns to this dish for the non-vegetarian.

Chinese Rice with Omelet Strips

This easy recipe turns leftover rice into a tasty and filling supper dish. You can use any leftover veggies you have in the fridge too.

Ingredients

Vegetable oil for cooking vegetables
Few drops of Sesame oil
1 clove garlic
Pinch Chinese five spice
A selection of vegetables
175g (6oz) cooked rice
Dash soy sauce
28g (1oz) butter
1 egg

Method

Heat both oils in a frying pan or wok. Finely chop the garlic and add to the pan. Add the five spice and vegetables and stir fry for 3-4 minutes. Keep stirring to prevent the vegetables sticking. Add a tablespoon or two of water and continue cooking for a further 2 minutes.

Add the rice and soy sauce and heat thoroughly.

Meanwhile melt the butter in an omelet pan or small frying pan. Beat the egg and add to the pan. Swirl until the egg until it covers the base of your omelet pan. Allow to cook until the egg is set and firm.

Turn out onto a plate and cut into strips.

Put the rice and veggies into your serving dish and arrange the omelet strips on top.

Cauliflower Cheese

This dish is delicious either on its own or as a side dish with a few new potatoes and a slice of ham for the meat eaters or a chunk of crusty bread.

Ingredients

10 cauliflower florets – fresh or frozen; it doesn't matter
Seasoning

For the sauce:

28g (1oz) butter
28g (1oz) flour
Milk
Grated cheese

Method

Cook the cauliflower florets in lightly seasoned water until tender. Drain and arrange in ovenproof dish. Keep warm and set aside.

For the sauce – this is a basic white sauce and can be used for lots of dishes (without the cheese)

Melt the butter in a saucepan over a medium heat then add the flour stirring continuously with a wooden spoon. It will look lumpy at first but it will come together; so don't panic!

Once the flour and butter are mixed together to a paste, begin to add the milk a bit at a time, stirring all the time. The mixture will thicken each time you add milk. Keep adding more milk whilst stirring until your sauce is at your desired thickness (I like mine quite thick). Add as much grated cheese as you like until it tastes good to you. Taste and season.

Pour your sauce over the cooked cauliflower and sprinkle a little grated cheese over the top. Put under the grill until golden brown. Serve immediately.

Note: If you want to make this in advance, don't grill the dish but cover and chill. When you want to use it, put in a pre-heated oven until the top is golden brown.

Vegetable Frittata

You could add bacon to this frittata to make a great dish for the non-vegetarian.

Ingredients (these are really just suggestions, you can use any leftover vegetables)

Broccoli split into florets
1 spring onion
Green beans
Zucchini
Dessertspoon frozen peas
Dessertspoon frozen corn kernels
2 eggs
1 tablespoon olive oil
Parmesan cheese (optional)
Seasoning

Method

Pre-heat the grill to its highest setting. Chop vegetables and cook in lightly salted water until soft then drain well and dry off on kitchen paper.

Heat the oil in a frying pan and sauté the drained vegetables for a few minutes.

Pour the beaten eggs into the pan with the vegetables, drawing the egg from the sides into the center, until set underneath.

Sprinkle with grated Parmesan and finish under the grill until the top is set and a lovely golden brown. Serve immediately.

Zucchini and Cod Fritters

Ingredients

1 egg
56g (2oz) cod
½ zucchini grated
Handful grated cheese
Flour
Seasoning
Olive oil
Small knob of butter

Method

Cut the cod into small, bite sized pieces. Whisk the egg well and add the cod, grated zucchini, grated cheese (if used) and salt and pepper to taste. Mix until well combined. Add enough flour to bring the mixture to a wet consistency that drops easily off the spoon.

Heat 2 tablespoons of olive oil in a frying pan. Carefully drop spoonfuls of the mixture into the pan and cook for around 4 minutes on each side. Towards the end of cooking, add the butter and spoon over the fritters to glaze.

These are delicious served with a crisp green salad.

Tomato Hash with a Kick

This is a great way to use up leftover potato and tomatoes. You could substitute the tomatoes for fish if you prefer.

Ingredients

1 onion
225g (8oz) cooked, floury potatoes
5-8 tomatoes
28g (1oz) butter
1 tablespoon chili oil
1 teaspoon tabasco sauce
1 tablespoon chopped parsley
Seasoning

Method

Peel and slice the onion. Cut potatoes into small dice.

Melt 18g of the butter in a frying pan and add the onion. Fry gently until softened but not browned, around 2-3 minutes. Add the chili oil and potatoes. Fry for around 7-8 minutes, turning occasionally until crisp and lightly browned. Add the tomatoes and remaining 10g of butter and cook for a further 2 minutes or until the tomatoes are soft.

Stir in the tabasco sauce, taste and season if required. Serve immediately. Delicious topped with a lightly poached egg.

Parsnip and Coconut Soup

This soup is a great standby to have in the fridge for when you need a quick supper. As this recipe only uses half a can of coconut milk, you can use some of the leftover milk in the 'Vegetable Skewers with Satay Sauce' recipe on the next page. Any left can be added to a curry.

Ingredients

3 parsnips
1 small onion
1 clove garlic
Half a can of coconut milk
Seasoning

Method

Peel and chop the parsnips and onion into small chunks. Boil in salted water until soft. Drain well. Put the parsnips and onion into a blender along with the crushed garlic and coconut milk. Blend until smooth adding extra milk if the soup is too thick.

Reheat and serve sprinkled with paprika and a chunk of buttered crusty bread.

Vegetable Skewers with Satay Sauce

Homemade vegetable skewers are much nicer than those you would get from any takeaway and really simple to make.

Ingredients

Assortment of Vegetables
1 dessertspoon olive oil
1 dessertspoon lemon juice

For the Satay Sauce

56g (2oz) smooth peanut butter
1 dessertspoon olive oil
1 dessertspoon hot water
1 dessertspoon light soy sauce
1 tablespoon apple juice
1 tablespoon coconut milk

Method

To make the satay sauce simply mix all your ingredients together.

Soak 4 wooden skewers in water for at least 15 minutes to prevent burning.

Cut your choice of vegetables into large chunks and thread onto the skewers. Mix the oil and lemon juice together and brush over the vegetables.

Preheat the grill and cook the skewers until the vegetables are cooked and slightly browned.

Serve hot with the satay sauce.

Puy Lentil and Mushroom Stuffed Peppers

Stuffed peppers are a great standby for if you have unexpected visitors. They take just minutes to prepare and look like you have gone to a lot of trouble. Delicious served with a crisp green salad or a few French fries.

Ingredients

1 Pepper – any color
56g (2oz) Puy Lentils
3 small tomatoes
1 clove garlic
Fresh basil leaves
1 shallot
1 tablespoon oil
Grated cheese

Method

Rinse dried Puy lentils to remove any debris.

Put the lentils into a pot of cold water so that they are covered by about 3 inches of water.

Bring the water up to the boil. As soon as it starts boiling, reduce the heat to a good simmer.

Simmer for 15-20 minutes, the Puy lentils should still have some bite to them. Drain well.

Cut top off the pepper and reserve for later. Scoop out the seeds and white core from the body of the pepper then blanch the pepper and top in boiling water for around 2 minutes. Remove and drain well.

Heat half the oil in a frying pan and add the crushed garlic and finely chopped shallot. Cook for a couple of minutes until the shallot is transparent. Chop the mushrooms finely and add to the shallot and garlic. Cook for a further 3 minutes. If you are using any other vegetables you should add them at this stage.

Remove from the heat and stir in the cooked puy lentils. Mix together well, taste and season to your liking.

Place your pepper in an oven-proof dish and half fill with the lentil mixture. Place two of the small tomatoes in the pepper then fill to top with the remaining lentil mixture. Place the top on the pepper. Drizzle with a little oil, loosely cover with foil and bake in a medium to hot oven for around 30 minutes or until cooked. Serve hot or cold.

Tabbouleh

This middle eastern dish is a lovely accompaniment to any fish or you could simply serve as a salad with crusty bread.

Ingredients

112g (4oz) couscous
2 tomatoes
¼ cucumber
1 bunch spring onions, sliced
28g (1oz) fresh parsley
Grated zest of a ½ lemon
3 tbsp olive oil
1 tbsp lemon juice
1 crushed garlic clove
125ml (4 fl oz) vegetable stock or water

Method

Put the couscous into a large bowl and pour over boiling water or vegetable stock and stir. Cover with cling film and leave to stand for 5 minutes until all the liquid has been absorbed. Separate the grains by stirring through with a fork.

Finely dice the tomatoes and the cucumber. Slice the spring onions and finely chop the parsley, then add everything to the couscous with the grated zest of a lemon.

Whisk the olive oil, lemon juice and the garlic with plenty of seasoning and drizzle over the couscous.

Sesame Noodle Stir-Fry

This is a tasty and very quick dish to prepare. It is best to prepare all your ingredients before beginning to cook as stir-frying is fast!

Ingredients

1 teaspoon red wine vinegar
1 tablespoon soy sauce
1 tablespoon tomato ketchup
2 tablespoons orange juice
1 teaspoon clear honey
1 teaspoon clear honey
1 tablespoon vegetable oil
Selection of vegetables; baby sweetcorn, peppers, spring onions, zucchini, carrot, spring cabbage etc.
42g (1½ oz) dried fine noodles
Teaspoon sesame seeds (optional)

Method

Combine the vinegar, soy sauce, tomato ketchup, orange juice and honey in a bowl. Add the cornflour and stir well.

Heat the oil in a non-stick frying pan and stir-fry your chosen vegetables for around 4-5 minutes. Add the cornflour mixture and bring to the boil stirring all the time. Reduce the heat and simmer for 1 minute or until the sauce is thickened.

Meanwhile cook the noodles as the directions on the packet. Drain and add to the pan of vegetables. Add sesame seeds, stir well.

Delicious either hot or cold.

Moroccan Style Stew

A fabulous dish for a cold winter evening. Serve with lightly steamed vegetables or just a few chunks of crusty bread.

Ingredients

1 dessertspoon virgin olive oil
1 clove garlic
1 small onion
Small can red kidney beans (200g)
10g fresh coriander
10g chopped mint
1 teaspoon chili powder
1 teaspoon ground cumin
1 small can chopped tomatoes (200g)
1 small can chickpeas (200g)
50g dried apricots
28g blanched almonds
Half vegetable stock cube

Method

Put oil, crushed garlic, chopped onion, herbs and spices into a saucepan and mix well. Cook over a medium heat for around 5 minutes.

Add all the remaining ingredients, making up the stock cube with a quarter of a pint of cold water. Bring to the boil and cook for around 20 minutes until the sauce is thickened.

Serve in a bowl with a sprinkling of fresh
herbs.

Some Simple Conversion Figures

Oven Temperatures

°C	°F	Gas
110	225	¼
120	250	½
140	275	1
160	325	3
180	350	4
200	400	6
220	425	7
240	475	9

Remember to always preheat your oven to the desired temperature.

Weights

1oz (ounce)	=	28g (gram)
1lb (pound)	=	454g
2.2046 lbs	=	1kg (kilo)

Liquid

1 fl oz	=	25 ml
3½ fl oz	=	100 ml
8 fl oz	=	250 ml
1 pint	=	600 ml
1¾ pints	=	1 ltr

Thank You

Thank you for buying this book and I really hope it has given you some inspiration for simple, economical and interesting vegetarian meals to prepare for yourself.

I don't pretend to be a professional chef but I do really love to cook for myself and hope you will be inspired to start to cook fresh, homemade meals rather than settle for the TV dinners from the freezer section of your supermarket.

Remember, most of these recipes can be adapted to your own personal taste by adding your own favorite ingredients. So be adventurous and change things around a bit – this is how family favorite recipes are actually born!

If you enjoyed this book I would really appreciate it if you would leave a review on Amazon. Simply type in the title and author in the search bar of Amazon and click on the book and leave your review. Thank you so much.

If you are interested in receiving notification of the next book in the 'Budget Cooking for One' series, please leave your email address at the address below.

www.eepurl.com/SZOLH

If you have any simple recipes for one that you would like to contribute to one of my upcoming books, please email me.

Penelope.Oates21@gmail.com

Upcoming Books in the 'Budget Cooking for One' series:

Crockpot Cooking for One
Simple Desserts for One
TV Snacks for One
Chicken Recipes for One
Breakfast Recipes for One

Thank you again.

Penny

Printed in Great Britain
by Amazon